LIVING WITH EVERGREENS

David H. Rosen

vincent tripi
foreword

art by Diane Katz

RESOURCE *Publications* • Eugene, Oregon

Rosenberry
books,
etc.

Also by David H. Rosen

Patient-Centered Medicine: A Human Experience

(with Uyen Hoang)

Lost in the Long White Cloud: Finding My Way Home

Time, Love and Licorice: A Healing Coloring Storybook

Clouds and More Clouds

The Tao of Elvis

(a Rosenberry Books/Wipf & Stock edition)

The Healing Spirit of Haiku

(with Joel Weishaus)

Evolution of the Psyche

(with Michael Luebbert)

The Tao of Jung: The Way of Integrity

Transforming Depression:

Healing the Soul Through Creativity

Medicine as a Human Experience

(with David Reiser)

Lesbianism: A Study of Female Homosexuality

ISBN: 978-1-5326-0854-4

Designed by Rosenberry books, etc.
101 Nicks Bend West
Pittsboro, NC 27312
800.723.0336 919.969.2767
www.rosenberrybooks.com
Rosenberry books, etc. is a registered trademark.

Wipf & Stock is an imprint of Wipf and Stock Publishers.
199 W. 8th Ave., Suite 3
Eugene, OR 97401
wipfandstock.com

Foreword

Yes, David Rosen has brought into the world a short book.

Short, but long on giving...long on pointing directly into the poet's heart.

Plenty of places for the reader to sit-in, to settle.

Feel the branches-roots-trunk-cones & sky as yourself!

vincent tripi
autumn 2016

LIVING WITH EVERGREENS

little poems by David H. Rosen, MD

art by Diane Katz

David Rosen

"The more I give to thee, the more I have"

William Shakespeare
Romeo and Juliet, Act II, Scene 2

Through the trees
a falling star

Call me one of
them evergreens

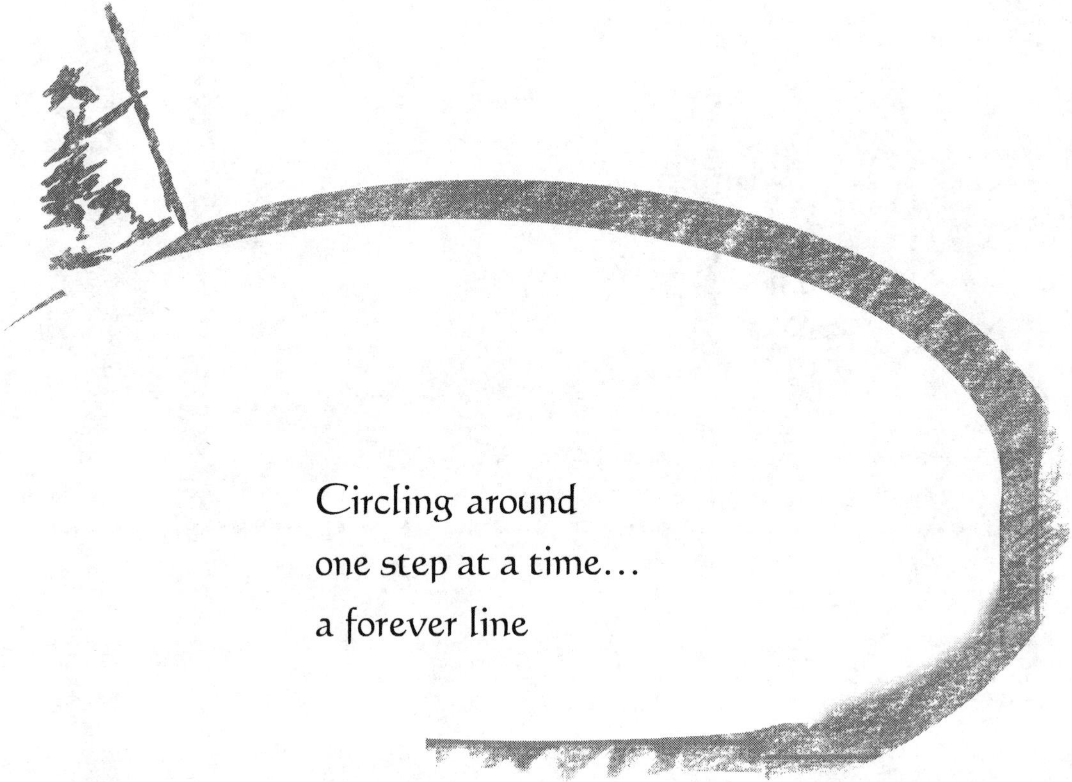

Circling around
one step at a time…
a forever line

Butterflies flutter by…
back to the dishes

Why do I laugh?
not far off —
tears

Red lentil sauce…
Happy Valentine's
Day

After making love...
eating red grapefruit

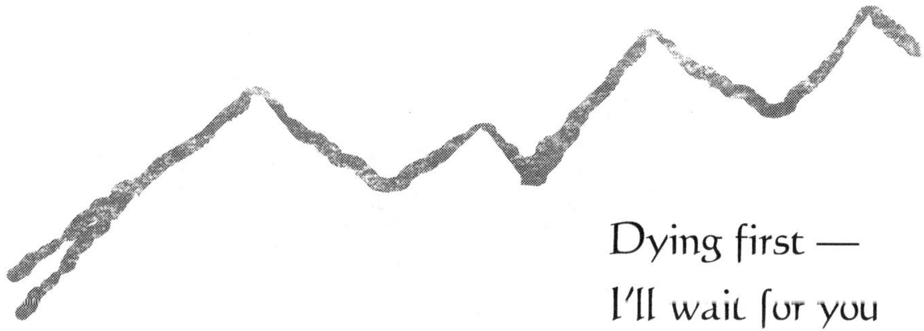

Dying first —
I'll wait for you
above or below

On Mother Earth —
crisp air
falling leaves

Tops of fir trees
swaying...
sound of water

Your bed, my cloud

Noisy
quiet…
reborn

Moving slowly —
white clouds
beyond the pines

Near autumn's end...
walking with my shadow
in the forest

Sipping local wine…
birds hurry home

Flock of graveyard
crows… no more
murder!

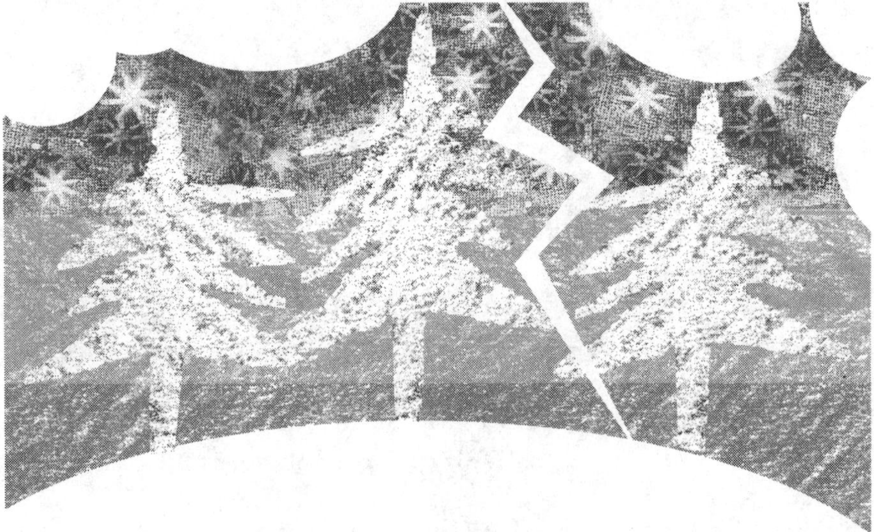

Surrounded by evergreens
grey clouds overhead —
lightning strikes

Sorrow hollow holy

Lone red cedar
on a bluff
Eden Falls

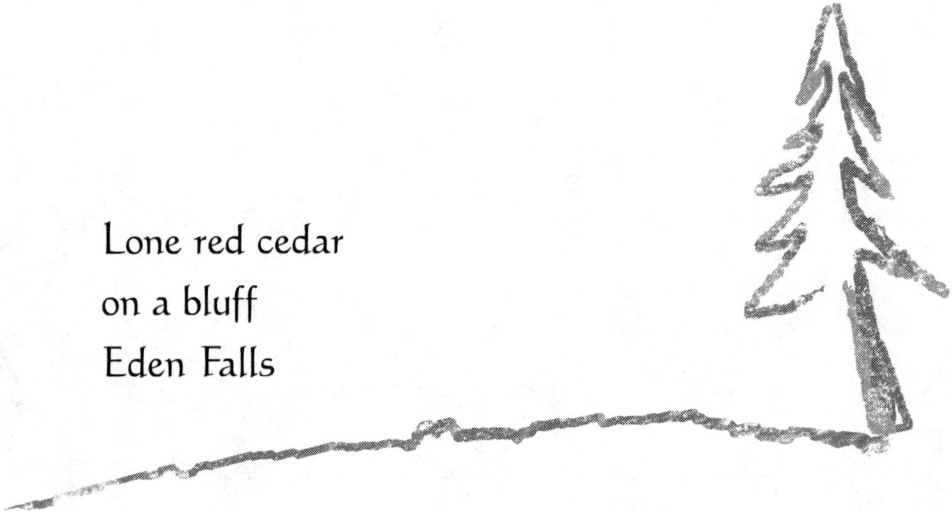

Three bears
out the window —
joy fills the room

Memories of Nihon…
emptiness, suchness,
fullness

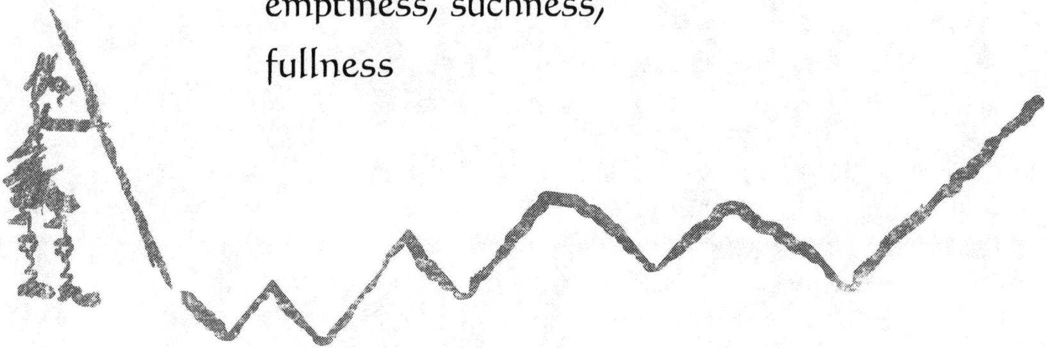

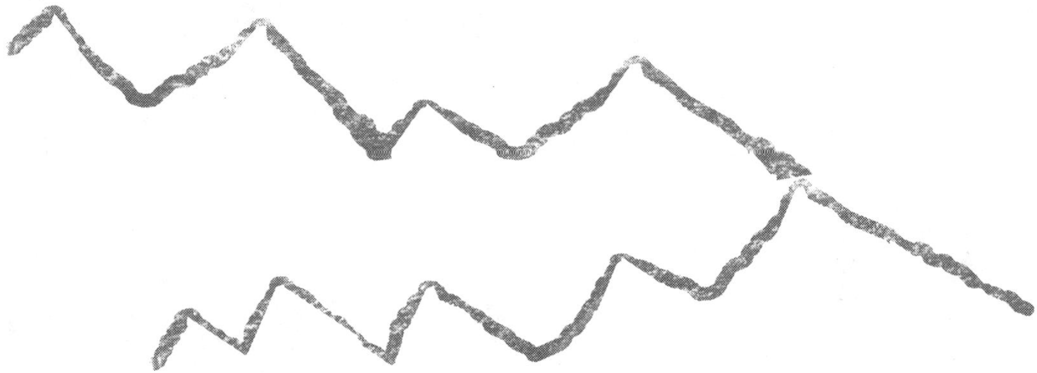

Lost Valley...
full of light, stone
green buds

Gigantic hills
trees ablaze…
snow blossoms of Spring

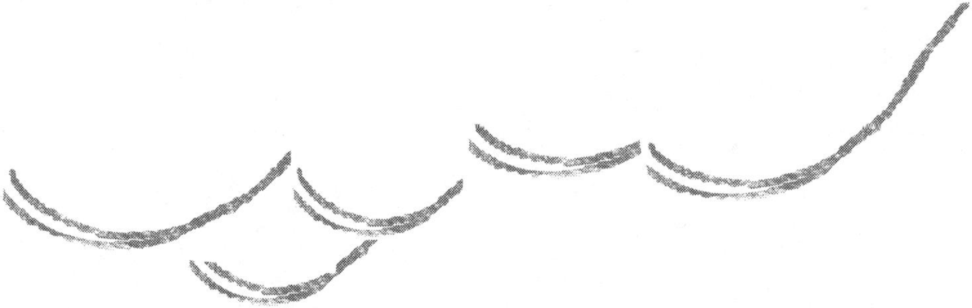

Green hills,
grey clouds…
gratitude

Flowing
Buffalo River...
cold jade water

Pitch black...
awakened by
a loon

Shimmering light…
windless
water

Cloud of pollen
drifts by…
a goddess

Hummingbird...
silence

Tears rain love

Vital
legacy…
love

David Rosen

About the Author

Dr David H. Rosen is a physician, psychiatrist, and Jungian analyst. His interests include: finding meaning in suffering; dreams; spirituality as it relates to healing; and all kinds of creativity.

David is the author of a dozen books, including *The Tao of Jung: The Way of Integrity*; *Transforming Depression: Healing the Soul through Creativity*; *Patient-Centered Medicine: A Human Experience* with Uyen Hoang; *Spelunking Through Life; Time, Love and Licorice: A Healing Coloring Storybook;* and *The Tao of Elvis*. Dr Rosen is editor of the Texas A&M University Press twenty-volume *Fay Book Series in Analytical Psychology.* David has contributed works to and edited the following anthologies: *Less is More: A Collection of Ten-Minute Plays* and *Darkness Holding Light: A Collection of Poems* by The Eugene Friends of Jung. Rosen's books have been translated into many languages.

David was born in 1945 in Port Chester, New York, and attended University of California, Berkeley and the University of Missouri School of Medicine. He received psychiatric training at the University of California, San Francisco and subsequent training in Jungian analysis. He was the initial holder of the McMillan Professorship in Analytical Psychology at Texas A&M University (the first of its kind in the world), and is now Affiliate Professor in Psychiatry at Oregon Health & Science University.

Currently living in Eugene, Oregon, with his wife Lanara, David walks, paints and sees analytic patients. He also creates visual art, performs stand-up comedy, and writes haiku, novelle and ten-minute plays.

About the Artist

Salvador Dali's Don Quixote continues to inspire Diane Katz's illustration of David Rosen's "little poems." *Living with Evergreens* follows the journey of David's haiku collection, *Spelunking Through Life*.

Diane has illustrated many books of haiku, including *Learning to See the Truth; The Stone House; Beneath the Willow Tree*; and *In the Night Shallows*, which are available from Rosenberry Books.

Diane also created artwork for David Rosen's *The Tao of Elvis* and *Time, Love and Licorice: A Healing Coloring Storybook.*

She is currently illustrating *The Whistle Prayer* and is the author of *On All My Holy Mountain: A Modern Fraktur; Apples Dipped in Honey: A Jewish ABC;* and *The Story-Letters from Appletta Tooth Fairy.*

Through Rosenberry Books, Diane's work has been seen at the Metropolitan Museum of Art, the Smithsonian, the Chicago Institute of Art, Washington National Cathedral, etc. and is recognized by Design Observer of the Winterhouse Institute.

Diane lives with her husband in the woods of North Carolina.

Also of interest from Rosenberry Books and Wipf & Stock:

The Tao of Elvis by David H. Rosen, MD

"Magnificent … Truly a work of art. It brings to mind the inspired illuminated manuscripts of the Middle Ages." — Sue Monk Kidd, author of *The Secret Life of Bees*. In a most readable fashion, Rosen illuminates the inner Elvis and the myth of Elvis. Sumptuously designed and illlustrated.

Time, Love and Licorice:
A Healing Coloring Storybook
by David H. Rosen, MD

The attic is a wondrous place. It is a place to fix things: Dad's workshop is there, and Henry's special corner, which hides his secret supply of building blocks. When his soldier father comes back changed, Henry's fantastic block towers are threatened by Dad's sudden outbursts.

But in the attic inspirations come, and repairs of all kinds are made…

The drawings of Henry's optimistic, creative and imaginative world create a safe space in which children and families can face the disruptions of Post-Traumatic Stress Disorder (PTSD).